"As a pastor, I get asked lots of questions. I'm approached by unbelievers seeking to understand the gospel, new believers unsure about next steps, and maturing believers wanting help answering questions from their Christian family, friends, neighbors, or coworkers. It's in these moments that I wish I had a book to give them that was brief, answered their questions, and pointed them in the right direction for further study. Church Questions is a series that provides just that. Each booklet tackles one question in a biblical, brief, and practical manner. The series may be called Church Questions, but it could be called 'Church Answers.' I intend to pick these up by the dozens and give them away regularly. You should too."

Juan R. Sanchez, Senior Pastor, High Pointe Baptist Church, Austin, Texas

"Where can we Christians find reliable answers to our common questions about life together at church—without having to plow through long, expensive books? The Church Questions booklets meet our need with answers that are biblical, thoughtful, and practical. For pastors, this series will prove a trustworthy resource for guiding church members toward deeper wisdom and stronger unity."

Ray Ortlund, President, Renewal Ministries

Does
God Love
Everyone?

Church Questions

Does God Love Everyone?, Matt McCullough

How Can I Find Someone to Disciple Me?, J. Garrett Kell

How Can I Love Church Members with Different Politics?, Jonathan Leeman and Andy Naselli

How Can Our Church Find a Faithful Pastor?, Mark Dever

How Can Women Thrive in the Local Church?, Keri Folmar

Is It Loving to Practice Church Discipline?, Jonathan Leeman

What If I Don't Desire to Pray?, John Onwuchekwa

What If I Don't Feel Like Going to Church?, Gunner Gundersen

What If I'm Discouraged in My Evangelism?, Isaac Adams

What Should I Do Now That I'm a Christian?, Sam Emadi

Why Should I Be Baptized?, Bobby Jamieson

Why Should I Give to My Church?, Jamie Dunlop

Why Should I Join a Church?, Mark Dever

Does God Love Everyone?

Matt McCullough

WHEATON, ILLINOIS

Does God Love Everyone?

Copyright © 2021 by 9Marks

Published by Crossway
      1300 Crescent Street
      Wheaton, Illinois 60187

Cover design: Jordan Singer

First printing 2021

Printed in the United States of America

Trade paperback ISBN: 978-1-4335-7215-9
ePub ISBN: 978-1-4335-7218-0
PDF ISBN: 978-1-4335-7216-6
Mobipocket ISBN: 978-1-4335-7216-6

Library of Congress Cataloging-in-Publication Data

Names: McCullough, Matthew, author.
Title: Does God love everyone? / Matt McCullough.
Description: Wheaton, Illinois : Crossway, [2021] | Series: Church questions | Includes bibliographical references and index.
Identifiers: LCCN 2020028963 (print) | LCCN 2020028964 (ebook) | ISBN 9781433572159 (trade paperback) | ISBN 9781433572166 (pdf) | ISBN 9781433572173 (mobi) | ISBN 9781433572180 (epub)
Subjects: LCSH: God (Christianity)—Love. | Trust in God.
Classification: LCC BT140 .M335 2021 (print) | LCC BT140 (ebook) | DDC 231/.6—dc23
LC record available at https://lccn.loc.gov/2020028963
LC ebook record available at https://lccn.loc.gov/2020028964

Crossway is a publishing ministry of Good News Publishers.

BP			30	29	28	27	26	25	24	23	22	21
15	14	13	12	11	10	9	8	7	6	5	4	3	2	1

For God so loved the world, that he gave his only Son, that whoever believes in him should not perish but have eternal life.

John 3:16

Do you believe that God loves everyone? If you do, you're in good company.

A few years ago, a group of researchers surveyed what people believed about God. Among many other interesting things, they found that three out of every four adults believe in a God or higher power who loves all people, regardless of their faults.

That's a big number no matter how you look at it. But what interests me most is how this belief about God remains high, straight across categories that normally divide us.

The percentage of women was slightly higher (82 percent), but still 72 percent of men believe that God loves everyone.

The sixty-five-and-older crowd was most likely to affirm God's love (83 percent), but so did 72 percent of those in their thirties and forties.

The more educated you are, the less likely you'll believe in a God of love, but 70 percent of those with a college degree still do.

Even half of the respondents with no religious affiliation at all believe there is a loving higher power.[1]

For all of our notable divisions, most people agree that God loves everyone.

Maybe you agree. Maybe you've always assumed God loves everyone, that it's basically his job to do so—that no matter how we might disagree with each other about what's right, we can at least depend on God loving us no matter what.

If that sounds like you, this booklet may surprise you.

Maybe, though, you're coming to this booklet from another perspective. Maybe you're asking whether God loves everyone because you can't imagine that God could love *you*. After all, you certainly don't love you, and you're not sure anyone else you know really does either. And if you were God, you wouldn't love someone like you.

If that's where you're coming from, this booklet will be surprising to you too.

Before we ask whether God loves everyone, there's another question we need to ask first: How can we even *know* if God loves everyone?

How Could You Know If God Loves Everyone?

This question is difficult for at least a couple reasons.

We Can't Know If God Loves Everyone from Paying Attention to Nature

Our world is full of delights; many of them we can enjoy without lifting a finger. The conditions

11

on earth seem finely tuned to support our lives. Signs of careful design surround us, as if our world were made by a creator who wanted us to thrive. We have air to breathe, food to eat, water to drink, and sunlight for warmth. We have bodies through which we enjoy the gifts the world offers us—bodies so complex that despite recent scientific advances, we still barely understand why they work as well as they do.

More than that, we have the ability to reflect, imagine, dream, and create. We're able to communicate with others, build friendships, and do good work together.

If one measure of love is the quality of the gifts showered on the beloved, there's plenty of evidence from nature that the maker of heaven and earth is a God of great love.

The problem is that nature sends us mixed messages. For all its beauty and goodness, our world is also marked by undeniable brutality and what seems like senseless suffering. The natural environment, so finely tuned for our thriving, sometimes turns against us.

A week before I began writing this booklet, a devastating tornado ripped through the heart of my city while most of us slept. It destroyed homes and businesses, injured hundreds, and killed over twenty people.

As I write, a virus that first gripped a city in China now stretches its fingers all around the world. Millions have contracted the disease. Hundreds of thousands have died.

Our bodies, so complex and high-functioning, are sometimes born compromised with no clear explanation. Even under the best of circumstances, they eventually break down and die.

Hovering over the beauty and brokenness in our experience of the world is an apparent randomness that raises haunting questions about what's behind it all. Why are some children born into abuse and neglect, while couples longing for kids suffer infertility and miscarriage? I don't know. That doesn't seem to come from love.

Let's assume there is a God who created the world and now rules over all. Does this God love *anyone*? How could you know for sure? No matter where you look or how hard, you won't get a straight answer from the natural world.

We Can't Trust Our Assumptions about Who God Is or What His Love Is Like

We must try to understand God like we try to understand any other person. If we assume other people are just like us, we'll always have a hard time getting to know them. It's the same with God. He's personal, not merely an idea or some philosophical system. If we want to know him, we can't simply assume he's like whatever our gut tells us.

Let me illustrate. I'm an expert on what I enjoy doing to unwind on a Saturday. If it's spring or summer, I like to hike or fish. If it's fall, I like to sit on my couch and watch football, stuffing my face with traditional tailgate foods. But how I want to use my free time isn't necessarily how my wife wants to use hers. She's a different person who enjoys different kinds of rest. She unwinds by working in the yard, digging in the garden, taking a nap, or even knocking out chores around the house. Besides the nap, none of these things seem remotely like rest to me.

My point: you won't understand another person by assuming they are like you. If you want to understand someone else, you have to listen to them, pay attention to them, and observe what they are like. And if that's true in human-to-human relationships, how much more must this be true when we're talking about understanding and getting to know God—someone fundamentally not like us?

God Needs to Tell Us What He's Like

For us to know whom God loves, God has to tell us. And that's exactly what Christians believe God has done in the Bible. He has spoken to us about who he is, not just so we can know about him, but so that we can know him.

What the Bible tells us about God's love is stunningly beautiful.

- God's love is distinctive, part of what sets him apart from all others. "There is no God like you, in heaven or on earth, keeping covenant and showing steadfast love to your servants who walk before you with all their heart" (2 Chron. 6:14).

- God's love is dependable, even in the midst of unspeakable pain. "The steadfast love of the LORD never ceases; his mercies never come to an end; they are new every morning; great is your faithfulness" (Lam. 3:22–23).

- God's love is distinctive and dependable because it's not a switch he turns off and on, but an essential part of what defines him. "God *is* love" (1 John 4:8).

If you believe that God is love, chances are, at some level, you've been influenced by the Bible.

But we must be careful. We can't hear the phrase "God is love" and then assume all of our own ideas about the meaning of love. If the Bible is our main source for knowing *that* God is love, we must let the Bible define *what it means* that God is love, from top to bottom. We've got to let the Bible teach us about God's love even if—especially if—what it says challenges our assumptions.

So what does the Bible say about whom God loves?

Does God Love Everyone?

In the Bible, God shows himself to us not through a list of bullet points, but through a compelling story woven from Genesis to Revelation. From beginning to end, this story is a love story. And to understand whom God loves, we'll have to follow the main themes of this story turn by turn.

Before we jump in, let me give you a little preview of what's ahead. What the Bible says about God's love is complicated. It tells us that yes, God does love everyone. But God does not love everyone in the same way. That's the answer I want to explain in the rest of this booklet: God loves everyone, but he does not love everyone in exactly the same way.

To unpack this, we need to consider five steps through the central story of the Bible.

1. God Loves God

John tells us that God *is* love (1 John 4:8). Not that God has love. Not that God shows love sometimes in some places. But rather God *is* love in his essence, all the way down to his core.

That means the love story at the heart of the Bible begins before the world was even created.

"In the beginning, God . . ." (Gen. 1:1). Those are the first words of the Bible. They have huge implications. In the beginning, there was God. And that God, the God who was there already, *is* love.

Now, here is the mind-bending truth behind John's simple and familiar little statement: Before the world existed at all—before sun or the moon or the stars, before the oceans or the mountains or the trees, before the fish or the birds or the animals or we humans—God was already a God of love. It's part of who he *is*, and there's never been a point when he didn't love someone.

But whom did he love before he created the world?

The first thing to know about God's love is that before God loves anyone else, and before there was anyone else *to* love, God loves himself.

My gut instinct is to pull back from that statement. It sounds gross. It seems beneath us, much less God. But it's really not, for a few reasons.

For one thing, God is not like you or me. He's a different kind of being altogether. His love for himself isn't narrow and inward like mine. The Bible teaches that God is one God in three persons—the Father, the Son, and the Holy Spirit. So when he loves himself, his love still moves "outward" from one person to another, for all of eternity. God loving himself looks like a father loving his son and a son loving his father in return, and on and on and on it goes, forever. Or as Jesus put it, praying to his Father, "You loved me before the foundation of the world" (John 17:24).

Of course, if I were to say that I love myself most of all, that *would* be gross. When we love ourselves, we're moving away from others. We're prioritizing our interests over theirs. For me and for you, self-love is selfish, alienating, and destructive. But when God loves himself, it's not like that. His love for himself is interpersonal, moving from person to person within the Trinity, self-giving not self-serving.

For another thing, God's love for God is appropriate. He's supremely lovable. Every trace of beauty, goodness, righteousness, and joy we've ever experienced comes from him. And every trace is just the faintest reflection of *his* own beauty, of who he is and has always been. There is nothing more joyous, more life-giving, more awe-inspiring than he is. When the Father looks at the Son he sees this beauty reflected, and he's delighted. When the Son looks at his Father, he too is delighted. Back and forth this delight— this insuppressible, unstoppable love—passes between them for all eternity. And it's only right that God should love himself. He's more worthy of love than anyone or anything else, just as my son is more worthy of my love than my favorite shoes.

There's one more reason God's love for God isn't a self-centered egomaniacal problem, which brings me to our second step through the Bible's love story.

2. God Loves Everyone

God's love for God feeds directly into God's love for me and for you.

Remember, before there was a world to love, God was already loving and already loved. He was not lonely. He didn't create the world, much less its humans, to fill some void in himself. He was eternally and perfectly happy, content, and self-sufficient.

Now maybe you're thinking that being needed by God doesn't sound so bad. Maybe you could stand to be needed and not being needed hurts a little bit. If I'm not needed, does that mean I'm dispensable and unimportant to him?

No, the fact that God didn't create us to fill some void in himself is the key to why our lives *do* matter so much.

Let's say God made you because he just simply couldn't live without you. That turns you into a commodity. In that case he manufactured you as a sort of crutch to lean on. It's just business, a simple transaction.

But precisely because God didn't need this world in order to be happy, or to know what love is, his motive for making us is not self-serving but self-giving. He didn't create us to take something from us. He created us to share the most life-giving, joyous gift in the universe—himself. He didn't create us because he had to. He created us because he wanted to. In other words, the God who is love created us for love. Your life matters because God chose you for life.

The story of creation in Genesis 1 begins with a poem that beautifully captures the comprehensiveness of God's work and the pleasure he took in it. Category by category, the writer lists the things God made. And after each day's work, we read the same response from God: "it was good." It was good. It was good. Day after day, it was good.

Then, at the crest of this building wave, we're brought into God's purpose for his finest work. Everything builds to this moment:

Then God said, "Let us make man in our image, after our likeness. And let them have dominion over the fish of the sea and over the birds of the heavens and over the livestock and over all the earth and over every creeping thing that creeps on the earth."

> So God created man in his own
>   image,
>   in the image of God he
>   created him;
>   male and female he created them.
>   (Gen. 1:26–27)

When God looks at the man and the woman, at those he has made in his own image, he sees something *very good*. This is a statement of his love. It applies to every human being—past, present, and future.

Love always involves delight in something. This is what I mean when I say that I love blue-grass music, or the novels of William Faulkner, or the taste of delicious smoked meat. Something about these things draws delight out of me. They please me. I love them.

According to Genesis 1, in God's eyes, every human made in his image is *very good*. Not an accident, not a mistake, not a disease on our planet, but an object of unique delight.

This is an affirmation of love. God loves everyone in the same way I love the summer's first slice of key lime pie, or the sound of my kids' laughter when they're tickled, or the sight of my wife's face in the morning. These things are very good. And in this way, God delights in every human life. It's his love that makes us human.

When we're talking about love between people, there's another dimension to love that comes out. Love involves giving of yourself in a way that's good for another. It's easy for me to say I love you. But is it love if you're in trouble and I do nothing? Is it love if you have a need that I can meet, but I hold back what's mine? You'd be right to wonder if I really love you. Love that won't lift a finger is mere sentimentality. True love is active.

In this sense too God loves everyone made in his image. It's from his love that he gives good gifts to his creatures.

Psalm 136 is a hymn that celebrates God's steadfast love. Each line gives an example of the good things God has done and is followed by the words "for his steadfast love endures forever." There are all sorts of examples from God's creation of the world to his redemption of Israel from Egypt to his gift of land to his people. But the final example looks beyond God's love for Israel and celebrates his love for everyone: God "gives food to all flesh, for his steadfast love endures forever" (Ps. 136:25).

Jesus picks up a similar theme in his Sermon on the Mount. He's telling the crowd that it's not enough for them to love their friends and families, the ones who are easy to love for one reason or another. They also should love their enemies. They should love everyone. And the reason for this call to love everyone is that their love should be like God's love. "But I say to you, 'Love your enemies and pray for those who persecute you, so that you may be sons of your Father who is in heaven. For he makes his sun rise on the evil and on the good, and sends rain on the just and on the unjust" (Matt. 5:44–45). God gives sun and rain to everyone, the good and evil, the just and unjust. That's because he loves everyone made in his image.

The existence of the world and every life within it only makes sense as part of a love story. But the beautiful beginning we've just considered only makes the story's dark turn, our next step, all the more heartbreaking.

3. No One Loves God

The opening chapters of Genesis describe not just the creation of the world but the beginning of a relationship. It gives us a glimpse into a relationship of love and trust between God and the humans he made in his image. And it shows us that this relationship of love and trust came protected by guardrails. The same love that gave life to Adam and Eve also gave them rules to obey, rules meant to protect them and their flourishing where God placed them.

At the root of everything that's broken in our good and beautiful world is a breakdown of trust in God's love and authority.

Genesis 3 tells us how Adam and Eve rejected God's rules. They chose to disobey him only after they were convinced that the rules he'd given them weren't good for them. In other words, they doubted God's love. Then trust gave way to rivalry. They decided their interests and his interests didn't line up, and they had to do what was right for them.

Whether we see it or not, you and I make the same decision every time we sin. Sin happens when we decide God's interests and our interests don't line up, when we decide we have to do what's right for us.

And the relational breakdown doesn't stop there. In both the story Genesis tells and our own experience, our broken relationship with God spreads into human relationships too. Immediately we see blame-shifting, envy, murder, and all forms of abuse and oppression (Genesis 3–4).

Psalm 14 sums up what the Bible says about how we humans have responded to our Creator who loves us.

> The LORD looks down from heaven on
>   the children of man,
>   to see if there are any who
>   understand,
>   who seek after God.
> They have all turned aside; together they
>   have become corrupt;
>   there is none who does good,
>   not even one. (vv. 2–3)

Without love for God to orient us, we turn aside to our own ways. We fill the world with individual, autonomous mini-gods wrestling back and forth for advantage. All hell breaks loose.

4. God Loves Sinners

God created us for love. We rejected his love. That could have been the end of this love story. In a way we could say that it should have been the end. For us it probably would have been.

But in fact it's God's response to his own rejection that shows us a depth of love we otherwise couldn't imagine.

John 3:16 may be the Bible's most familiar statement about God's love:

> For God so loved the world, that he gave
> his only Son, that whoever believes in him
> should not perish but have eternal life.

When I read "world," my first thought is of scale. God loves everyone in the whole world. Of course that's true in the sense we talked about before. But that isn't what John means when he uses "world."

For him "world" is usually a reference to quality, not quantity. Or as one New Testament professor puts it, "*World* in John does not so much refer to bigness as to badness. In John's vocabulary, *world* is primarily the moral order in willful and culpable rebellion against God."[2]

When we get John's meaning we should be shocked. Not only does God love everyone as he made them, with the dignity and worth he designed for them, after his own image. God also loves everyone as they are—rebels against his loving authority, mini-gods who want their own ways rather than his.

John makes the same point in his letters. What does it mean that "God is love" (1 John 4:8)? Well, look at what John says next:

> In this the love of God was made manifest among us, that God sent his only Son into the world [think badness, not bigness], so that we might live through him. In this is love, not that we have loved God but that he loved us and sent his Son to be the propitiation for our sins. (1 John 4:9–10)

Do you see what John is showing us? God's love for the world comes first. He loved us when no one is asking for it and when no one would have been grateful to have it. He loved us and therefore sent his Son as a sacrifice to save sinners. And though the word "love" typically focuses on badness, not bigness, John also tells us this offer of forgiveness is for everyone, strong enough to cover "the sins of the whole world" (1 John 2:2).

In love, God sent his Son to rescue those who wanted nothing to do with him, and to restore the broken relationship of love.

This offer of rescue and restoration is an offer made with no exception. "For everyone who calls on the name of the Lord will be saved" (Rom. 10:13).

But this is the place to say that though God loves everyone, he does not love everyone in the same way. It is only "whoever believes in him" (God's Son, Jesus) who will "not perish but have eternal life" (John 3:16). There is a special love that he has for those who trust Jesus. It's the love of God for his redeemed people. And the Bible tells us that with this love there is an inside and an outside.

5. God Loves His People

It's impossible to understand the overarching story of the Bible without recognizing God's intention to set apart a unique people, uniquely his and uniquely loved.

Back in Genesis, after the world has been so badly spoiled by sin and selfishness, God calls one man, Abram (later called Abraham), and promises to bless him and make his descendants a great nation. The Lord said to him, "I will make of you a great nation, and I will bless you and make your name great, so that you will be a blessing. I will bless those who bless you, and him who dishonors you I will curse, and in you all the families of the earth shall be blessed" (Gen. 12:2–3).

Once Abraham's descendants grew into the nation of Israel, God again and again reaffirmed his special love for them among all the peoples of the earth. As he was giving his law to Israel, he reminded them, "Behold, to the LORD your God belong heaven and the heaven of heavens, the earth with all that is in it. Yet the LORD set his heart in love on your fathers and chose their offspring after them, you above all peoples, as you are this day" (Deut. 10:14–15). Everything and everyone belongs to the Lord, but he set his special love on this nation above all peoples.

God's special relationship with Israel serves as a picture of his relationship to the church.

The New Testament describes this relationship using the same sort of language, making sure we see it's a special and unique relationship of love.

Paul opens his letter to the Ephesians by praising God for setting his love on this new congregation, even before the foundation of the world:

> Blessed be the God and Father of our Lord Jesus Christ, who has blessed us in Christ with every spiritual blessing in the heavenly places, even as he chose us in him before the foundation of the world, that we should be holy and blameless before him. In love he predestined us for adoption to himself as sons through Jesus Christ, according to the purpose of his will, to the praise of his glorious grace, with which he has blessed us in the Beloved. (Eph. 1:3–6)

Near the end of this same letter, Paul compares the love of Christ for the church to the love of a husband for his wife: "Husbands, love your wives, as Christ loved the church and gave himself up for her" (Eph. 5:25).

This analogy to marriage is a big help for understanding the special love God has for his people. It's something like the love I have for my wife.

Of course there are many women that I love. I've got a mom and three sisters. I've got close female friends. I've got many sisters in Christ who belong to our church. I love all of them. But there is what you might call a discriminating love that I have for my wife. I love her in a way I don't love any other woman. That's how God loves his people.

But why, though? What is it about his people that God loves? That's the all-important question. If this special love has an inside and an outside—meaning, there are some he loves this way and some he does not—how do you get on the inside? This is where the Bible's message about God's love is most surprising.

God Doesn't Love His People Because They're Special

It would be natural to assume that God's special love for his people comes from something special about his people, something they've got that no one else does. But listen to how Deuteronomy explains why God made Israel "his treasured possession" out of all the peoples on earth:

> It *was not because* you were more in number than any other people that the LORD set his love on you and chose you, for you were the fewest of all peoples, but *it is because* the LORD loves you and is keeping the oath that he swore to your fathers. (Deut. 7:7–8)

Paul says something similar about God's love for the church. Writing to new Christians in Corinth, where they were especially tempted to try to one-up one another, Paul reminds them, "not many of you were wise according to worldly standards, not many were powerful, not many were of noble birth" (1 Cor. 1:26). Translation: you guys weren't winners. You weren't the popular crowd of chiseled athletes and beauty queens.

No. When the Lord set his love on his people, it wasn't because they were obviously his most desirable option. It's not as if the relationship began with a dating app, where God swiped his way through the profiles until he found the perfect match. Not even close. He "set his love on you . . . because the Lord loves you." He loves them because he loves them. That was true with Israel, and it's true for the church too.

God Doesn't Love His People Because They're Good

It would perhaps be even more natural to assume that God chooses his people based on whether or not they follow the rules. That sort of preference is a common feature in other religions—the insiders are the ones who earn it, the ones who deserve to be there. You only get what you can pay for.

Yet that's not how God relates to his people.

Of course obedience, what the Bible calls righteousness, matters to God. He wouldn't be who he is—he wouldn't be worthy of worship and trust—if he didn't see the difference between good and evil. The righteousness that God loves is not some set of arbitrary rules laid down to trap the unsuspecting or weed out the weak. The righteousness he loves reflects his own perfect commitment to what's right. God's righteousness is beautiful. It's worthy. And in our gut, not perfectly but still truly, we want a God who loves righteousness because we want a God opposed to injustice. And God does indeed love righteousness.

But God loves his people despite their persistent lack of righteousness.

Take the story of Israel, for example. The only theme in that story as consistent as God's steadfast love for Israel is the theme of Israel's forgetfulness, ingratitude, and preference for the gods of their neighbors.

The best illustration I know of for the character of God's people comes from the prophet Hosea. God himself designs an object lesson to capture what it's like for him to love Israel. He commands Hosea to marry a prostitute named Gomer, to love her and build his life around her despite her past. That's what Hosea does. But their wedding day isn't the story's happy ending.

Gomer leaves her marriage to return to prostitution. She prefers life as a whore to life as Hosea's wife. That's how God depicts Israel's treatment of him. That's whom he loves as his people.

God's new covenant people, the church, is made up of individuals who were no more righteous than Israel when God first set his love on them. Listen to how Paul describes the life of every Christian before God's love intervenes:

> For we ourselves were once foolish, disobedient, led astray, slaves to various passions and pleasures, passing our days in malice and envy, hated by others and hating one another. But when the goodness and loving kindness of God our Savior appeared, he saved us, not because of works done by us in righteousness, but according to his own mercy. (Titus 3:3–5)

Slaves to passion, just like Gomer. Disobedient, just like Israel. There was no cleanup effort, no "works done in righteousness," to draw out God's affection. His loving kindness came first, right down into the mess we had made of our lives.

God Loves His People through His Son

The difference between the inside and the outside of God's special love for his people comes down to Jesus. It's not a contest you win. It's not a status you earn. It's a gift you receive. And it comes only when you walk through the gate that Jesus opens for you.

> I am the way, and the truth, and the life. No one comes to the Father except through me. (John 14:6)

God sets his special love on unrighteous people not because he decided to *set aside righteousness*, but because he decided to *make his people righteous*. This is, as the old hymn beautifully puts it, "love to the loveless shown that they might lovely be."[3]

The story of Hosea and Gomer doesn't end with their marriage, but neither does it end in adultery and abandonment. It ends with an act of almost unimaginable mercy. God commands Hosea, this broken-hearted and betrayed husband, to go after his faithless wife and buy her back from the slavery she had chosen for herself. The slavery she had preferred to his companionship and care.

One pastor describes Hosea's story as "an anticipation in pageant form of Christ's story."[4]

It's not a stretch to imagine this story on Paul's mind in his letter to the Ephesians, when he describes Christians as those who "once lived in the passions of our flesh, carrying out the desires of the body and the mind, and were by nature children of wrath, like the rest of mankind" (Eph. 2:3). We were once, each one of us, Gomer. "But God, being rich in mercy, because of the great love with which he loved us, even when we were dead in our trespasses, made us alive together with Christ" (Eph. 2:4–5).

A little later on, like Hosea before him, Paul pictures this whole process as a marriage. He tells husbands to love their wives "as Christ loved the church and gave himself up for her" (Eph. 5:25). And the reason Christ gave himself for his bride was "that he might sanctify her, having cleansed her by the washing of water with the word, so that he might present the church to himself in splendor, without spot or wrinkle or any such thing, that she might be holy and without blemish" (Eph. 5:25–27).

Holy and blameless. That's what Christ wants for his bride. Righteousness still matters. But the righteousness of God's people—the righteousness God loves, that he delights to see—will come to them as a gift from his hand, a gift purchased for them by the blood of his Son.

Just as Hosea paid the price to redeem his unfaithful wife, so in Christ God paid what it cost to account for the sin of his people and to make them righteous.

That's what Paul means when he says Jesus "gave himself" for his church (Eph. 5:25).

That's what Peter means when he says "Christ also suffered once for sins, the righteous for the unrighteous, that he might bring us to God" (1 Pet. 3:18).

That's what Jesus himself meant when he said that he came to "give his life as a ransom for many" (Mark 10:45).

And it's an exchange perhaps best summed up in 2 Corinthians 5:21: "For our sake he [meaning God] made him [meaning Jesus] to be sin who knew no sin, so that in him we might become the righteousness of God."

Christians often describe God's love as unconditional. And that's true. God loves his people despite their sin against him. He loves them before they love him back, and before there's anything in them worthy of his love. Thanks be to God, that's all true.

But his love doesn't stop there. It gets far better than that. The Bible tells us God loves his people *in* Christ. In love the Father sends his Son to take on himself what his people deserve—the unrighteousness that God does not love and is bound to punish. That's why Christ died. But in Christ, God's people also take on what he deserves—the perfect, steadfast, unending love of God for his righteous Son.

It's a mystery we can't hope to fully grasp. But God's love for his people is an extension of the perfect, eternal love for his Son. On the night that he was betrayed, praying to his Father for the safety of those he was about to redeem, Jesus pulls back the veil and reveals to us the unthinkable mystery of the gospel.

The glory that you have given me I have
given to them, that they may be one even
as we are one, I in them and you in me,
that they may become perfectly one, so
*that the world may know that you sent
me and loved them even as you loved me*
. . . I made known to them your name,
and I will continue to make it known,
that *the love with which you have loved
me may be in them*, and I in them. (John
17:22–23, 26)

To be in Christ is to live in the love the Father
has for his Son. It's not simply that God loves his
people despite their sin. He loves them *because*
his Son is righteous. He loves them "even as" he
loves Jesus. The love with which he has loved his
Son is now "in them." When God looks on his
people, he sees the righteousness of his Son and
he is delighted in them.

So Where Does That Leave You?

For most of this booklet I've been trying to answer one big question: Does God love everyone?

The short answer the Bible gives us is that God loves everyone but not in the same way.

But the Bible was not written merely to inform us. It was written to invite us into relationship with the God who speaks to us in its pages. I want to finish by asking you to think about what the Bible's answer means for you.

At the beginning of this booklet I suggested that what I'd say about God's love might surprise you. Here's what I had in mind.

On one hand, maybe you've always assumed God loves everyone. That's what most people believe. Maybe you've just gone with the flow. And if you have, it could be that the way you've thought about God's love has actually been an excuse not to pay much attention to him at all. *Of course God loves everyone! That's his job. He'll be there when I need him. In the meantime, I'm gonna live my life on my terms.*

If that's how you've thought of God's love, you have reason to be concerned. He does not love everyone in the way that you've assumed. God's love is holy. Yes, his love is free-flowing, never-ending, and available to absolutely anyone. No, he is not stingy with his affection. But this love that is free is also demanding—to live inside the special love of God for his people, we have to repent of what we've loved more than him, and trust everything to his Son Jesus. He is the way, the truth, and the life. No one comes to God except through him.

On the other hand, perhaps you came to this booklet convinced that there's no way God could love everyone, because there's no way God could love you. Maybe your deeper question was really, does God love *me*? Could God love me?

By now I hope the surprising answer to that question, the answer God has given you in his word, is crystal clear.

Yes, God loves you because you are made in his image. He has given your life a dignity he hasn't given to any other sort of creature. And you experience his love for you every day. You have breath in your lungs. You have clothes on your back. You have food in your belly. And you have all that you have because God gives of himself to those he loves.

Yes, God loves you because he loves sinners. Despite your sin against him, he loves you still. He loves you so much that he gave his only Son so that if you believe in him you won't perish but have eternal life. In fact, you are reading this invitation to trust in him right now because he loves you.

If you believe in Jesus, if you trust in him rather than in anything you might do to save yourself, then God loves you even as he loves his own Son. That love is a burning, white hot, immoveable love you could never earn. It's a love that Christ has earned on your behalf. God loves you because when he looks at you, he sees Jesus. Not the weakness that so often disappoints you. Not the failures that so often let others down. That's not who you are to him if you're in Christ. The perfect righteousness of the only Righteous One covers you completely.

Now, what's left for you? You should rest in God's love for you.

This is easier said than done. There is something deep inside of us that would rather deserve what we get. We'd rather win merit badges than participation trophies.

Yet we can't possibly get the righteousness God loves that way. We have to accept something that somebody else deserves, and that's humbling. We cannot take credit for the love God gives us in Christ. We must give up on boasting. But what we get in exchange is a security we won't find anywhere else, as rock-solid as the eternal love of the Father for his Son. And a love you cannot earn is a love you can't lose. Rest in that love.

Recommended Resource

D. A. Carson, *The Difficult Doctrine of the Love of God* (Wheaton, IL: Crossway, 2000).

Notes

1. "When Americans Say They Believe in God, What Do They Mean?" Pew Research Center, April 25, 2018, https://www.pewforum.org/2018/04/25/when -americans-say-they-believe-in-god-what-do-they -mean/.
2. D. A. Carson, *The Difficult Doctrine of the Love of God* (Wheaton, IL: Crossway, 2000), 17.
3. Samuel Crossman, "My Song Is Love Unknown," 1664.
4. James Montgomery Boice, *The Minor Prophets*, vol. 1 (Grand Rapids, MI: Baker, 1983), 14.

Scripture Index

Genesis
1...................... 22, 24
1:1...................... 18
1:26–27............... 23
3–4...................... 27
12:2–3............... 32

Deuteronomy
7:7–8................. 35
10:14–15............. 32

2 Chronicles
6:14.................... 15–16

Psalms
14:2–3................. 28
136:25................. 25

Lamentations
3:22–23.............. 16

Matthew
5:44–45.............. 25–26

Mark
10:45................. 41

John
3:16.................... 29, 31
14:6.................... 39
17:22–23............. 43
17:24................. 19
17:26................. 43

Romans
10:13................. 31

1 Corinthians
1:26.................... 35

2 Corinthians
5:21.................... 41–42

Ephesians
1:3–6................. 33
2:3...................... 40

2:4–5 40
5:25 .... 33, 40, 41
5:25–27 40–41

Titus
3:3–5 38

1 Peter
3:18 41

1 John
2:2 31
4:8 .... 16, 18, 30
4:9–10 30

IX **9Marks**

Building Healthy Churches

9Marks exists to equip church leaders with a biblical vision and practical resources for displaying God's glory to the nations through healthy churches.

To that end, we want to see churches characterized by these nine marks of health:

1. Expositional Preaching
2. Gospel Doctrine
3. A Biblical Understanding of Conversion and Evangelism
4. Biblical Church Membership
5. Biblical Church Discipline
6. A Biblical Concern for Discipleship and Growth
7. Biblical Church Leadership
8. A Biblical Understanding of the Practice of Prayer
9. A Biblical Understanding and Practice of Missions

Find all our Crossway titles and other resources at 9Marks.org.

The Church Questions Series

For more information, visit **crossway.org**.